Self-Control in the Bible

Written by:
Sunny Kang

Illustrated by:
Alexandro Ockyno

E-Book: 978-1-7378681-2-5
Paperback: 978-1-7378681-3-2
Hardcover: 978-1-7378681-4-9

Self—control will protect you like strong walls around a city!

To :

From :

Date :

What is Self-Control?

Self-control is being able to control your own thoughts and actions.

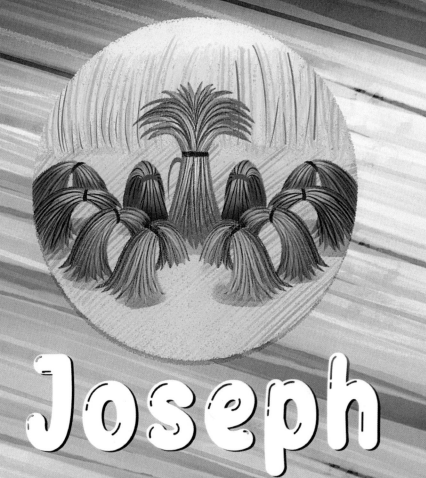

Joseph

The LORD was with Joseph,
and he became a successful man,
and he was in the house of his Egyptian master.

–Genesis 39:2–

Jacob had 12 sons and 1 daughter.
Joseph was son number eleven.
Joseph's mother was Rachel.
God gave Joseph dreams and also the ability
to know what they mean.

Joseph's older brothers did not like him
because Jacob loved Joseph the most.
Also Joseph had dreams of sheaves of grain and stars bowing down to him.
His older brothers knew it meant they would bow to him one day.
This made them angry.

So the brothers decided to send Joseph away.
Joseph was taken to Egypt as a servant and even became a prisoner.
But one day he became a powerful leader under Pharaoh.
Joseph protected many people and was very blessed.

Many years later,
Joseph's brothers came to Egypt because they needed grain.
They came to Joseph for help, but did not know it was him.
When Joseph saw them, he did not get angry.
He fed them and gave them extra gifts.

Joseph tested them, but eventually blessed them with food, sheep to shepherd, and a home to live in.
He even met his father Jacob again.
Joseph showed self-control by not hurting his brothers, but serving them.

Daniel

Then the king
gave Daniel high honors and many great gifts,
and made him ruler over the whole province of Babylon.

-Daniel 2:48-

There was once a king in a faraway land named Nebuchadnezzar.
He came and took over Jerusalem.
He also chose the smartest students and taught them his ways.
They all were bright students,
but none were brighter than Daniel and his three friends.

Their teacher gave Daniel and his three friends great teachings and food.
Their teacher wanted them to eat and drink everything he gave them.
However, God did not want them to eat certain foods and drinks.

After ten days,
Daniel and his three friends were healthier than the other students!
Daniel showed self-control by following God
and talking nicely to his teacher.
And God was with him.

Esther

The king loved Esther more than all the women,
and she won grace and favor in his sight more than all the virgins.

-Esther 2:17-

Queen Esther told Mordecai to have everyone fast
and pray for three days. She was going to talk to the king.
They both knew maybe God made her queen for this reason.

She approached the king, and the king was pleased.
King Xerxes asked what she wanted.
Queen Esther asked the king and Haman to come
to two great feasts she prepared.

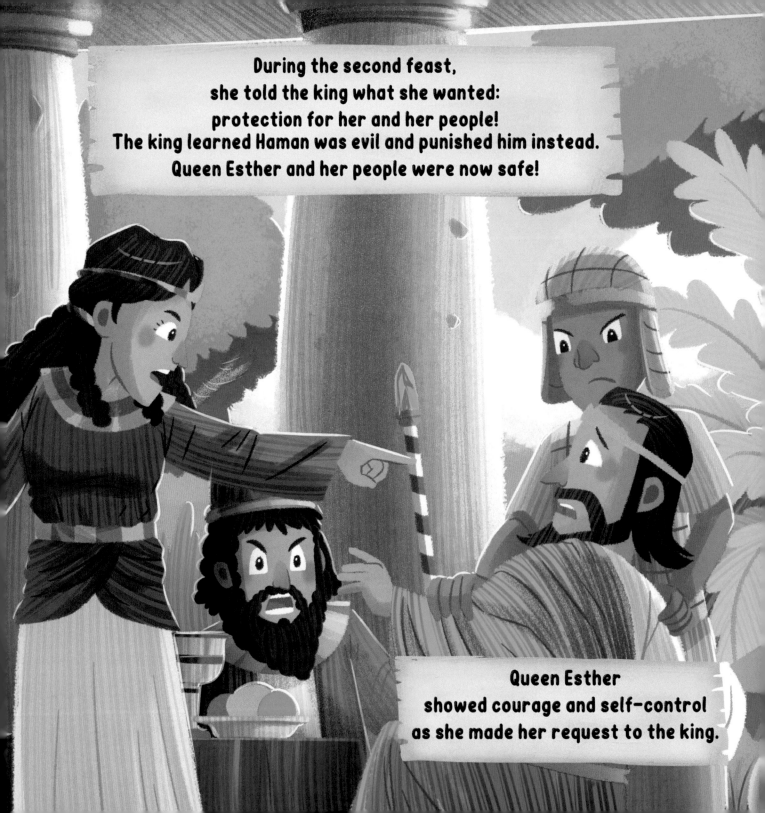

Nehemiah

If it pleases the king,
and if your servant [Nehemiah] has found favor in your sight,
send me to Judah, to the city of my fathers, that I may rebuild it.

-Nehemiah 2:5-

The walls and gates of his motherland,
Jerusalem, were destroyed.
This made it dangerous
for anyone living there.

One day,
the king asked him why he was sad and what he wanted.
Nehemiah wanted to rebuild the walls of Jerusalem.
The king allowed him to go and gave him all the help he needed!

When Nehemiah got to the city and started to rebuild the walls, there were people who tried to stop them.
They tried to scare the people to stop building.
But Nehemiah prayed, and God gave them courage.

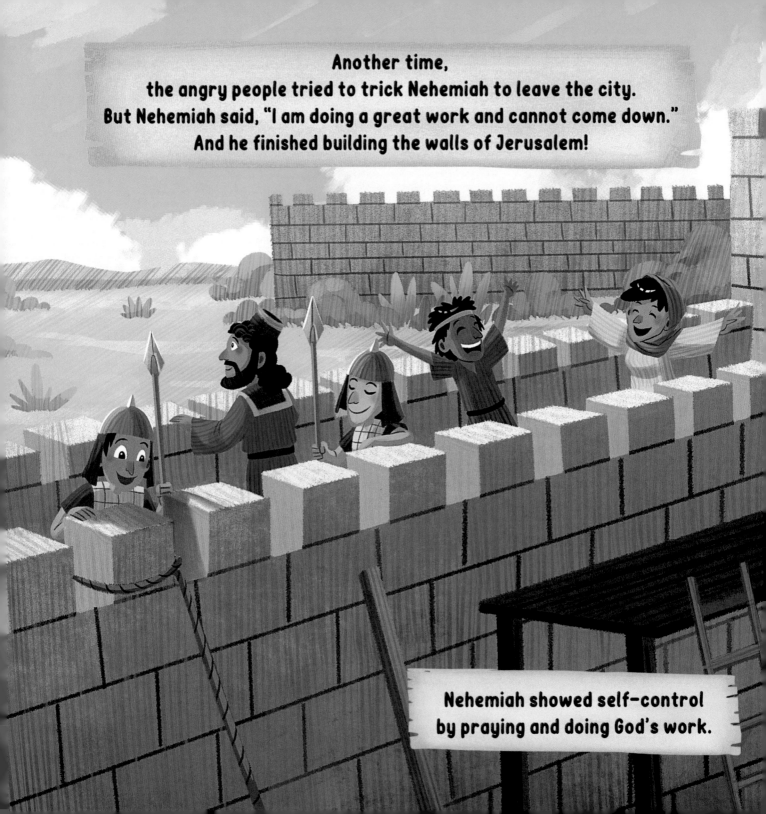

Another time,
the angry people tried to trick Nehemiah to leave the city.
But Nehemiah said, "I am doing a great work and cannot come down."
And he finished building the walls of Jerusalem!

Nehemiah showed self-control
by praying and doing God's work.

Jesus

So Jesus said to them,
"Truly, truly, I say to you, the Son can do nothing of his own accord,
but only what he sees the Father doing."

-John 5:19-

Jesus was the best example of self-control.
He had such a close relationship with God.
Jesus knew the best way to live and act.

Jesus enjoyed being alone with God.
It was very enjoyable and peaceful.
Early in the mornings, Jesus prayed, sang songs,
and enjoyed spending time with God.

Jesus also enjoyed serving, teaching, and helping others.
He knew He was not supposed to be alone with God all the time.
He came to show us the best way to live—
God's ways!

One time, Jesus was on top of a mountain spending time with God, Moses, and Elijah.
He was so close to God, his clothes became whiter and brighter than anything people have seen!

Peter was there too, and he was amazed.
He even wanted to stay in such a wonderful place.

But Jesus knew he had
to go back down the mountain and serve God's children.
He showed self-control by spending time alone with God
and by spending time helping people.

How Can
We Grow More Self–Control?

Ask Jesus into your heart!

Believe everything Jesus says!

Choose to follow Jesus every day!

Do you believe
in Jesus as your Lord and Savior?

About CornerStone Christian Academy & Tykes Preschool

Ms. Amy Benson,
Tykes Pre-School
Director

CornerStone Christian Academy & Tykes Preschool exists to encourage the development of the whole child engaging the student's spiritual, academic, and physical growth. It is our desire as followers of Christ, to pursue excellence in all that we do.

Our curriculum centers on Christ, Social & Emotional Learning, and age appropriate subject matters. The book you hold in your hands is an example of the biblical values we teach our students.

For More Information:
Website: www.ccanv.com
Instagram: @cornerstone_lv
Facebook: @lvcornerstone2

About the Author and Illustrator

Author
Sunny Kang is a Christ follower, husband, father, teacher, preacher, and author. He has pastored for over 10 years, serving as children's pastor for several of those years. He enjoys learning, meeting new people, communicating God's Word, superhero movies, and boba! He, his wife, and 2 sons live and serve in Las Vegas.

Follow Author:
Facebook: @AuthorSunnyKang
Instagram: @AuthorSunnyKang
Newsletter: http://bit.ly/authorsunnykang

Illustrator
Alexandro Ockyno is a full time freelance illustrator, living in Bali for almost 9 years. A happy man with a beautiful girlfriend, his dream is to create many children's books and share God's blessings with many others.

Follow Illustrator:
Facebook: @alessandro.altobelly
Instagram: @catandsashimi

Thank you
and hope you enjoyed this 3rd book
in the "Seeds to Trees" series!

DOWNLOAD YOUR FREE GIFT HERE!

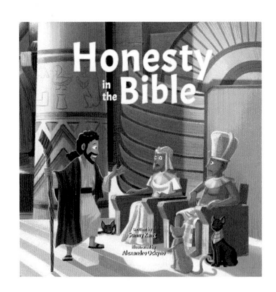

Link: bit.ly/Honesty-in-the-Bible-Free

Made in the USA
Columbia, SC
04 October 2021